Witness to History

Afghanistan

David Downing

Heinemann
LIBRARY

www.heinemann.co.uk/library

Visit our website to find out more information about **Heinemann Library** books.

To order:

☎ Phone 44 (0) 1865 888066

🗎 Send a fax to 44 (0) 1865 314091

💻 Visit the Heinemann Bookshop at www.heinemann.co.uk/library to browse our catalogue and order online.

First published in Great Britain by Heinemann Library,
Halley Court, Jordan Hill, Oxford
OX2 8EJ, part of Harcourt Education.
Heinemann is a registered trademark of
Harcourt Education Ltd.

© Harcourt Education Ltd 2004
First published in paperback in 2005
The moral right of the proprietor has been asserted.

Produced for Heinemann by Discovery Books Ltd
Editorial: Gillian Humphrey, Nancy Dickmann and
Tanvi Rai
Design: Rob Norridge and Ron Kamen
Picture Research: Rachel Tisdale
Production: Séverine Ribierre

Originated by Dot Gradations
Printed and bound in China
by South China Printing Company

ISBN 0 431 17064 9 (hardback)
08 07 06 05 04
10 9 8 7 6 5 4 3 2 1

ISBN 0 431 17069 X (paperback)
09 08 07 06 05
10 9 8 7 6 5 4 3 2 1

British Library Cataloguing in Publication Data
Downing, David, 1946–
  Afghanistan. – (Witness to History)
  958.1

A full catalogue record for this book is available from the
British Library.

Acknowledgements
The publishers would like to thank the following for
permission to reproduce photographs: Bettmann/Corbis
p.16, 19; Corbis pp. 7 (Peter Turnley), 10 (Ric Ergenbright),
12 (Barnabas Bosshart), 22 (Reza/Webistan), 24 (Peter
Turnley), 28 (Reza/Webistan), 32 (Francoise de Mulder), 33
(Baci), 38 (Webistan/Zaheeruddin); Corbis Sygma pp. 6
(Bisson Bernard), 30 (Patrick Durand), 39 (Bisson Bernard),
40 (Stephane Ruet), 43 (Ron Sachs); Popperfoto pp. 14, 18,
26, 31, 50, 51; Popperfoto/Reuters pp. 34 (Peter Greste),
36, 42, 44, 45, 47; Topham/Associated Press p. 20;
Topham/ImageWorks pp. 4, 9, 35; Topham/Photri p. 48.

Cover photograph shows an Afghan woman and child
walking past a tank in Kabul in 1989. Reproduced with
permission from Topham.

The publishers would like to thank Bob Rees, historian and
Assistant Head Teacher, for his assistance in the
preparation of this book.

Words appearing in the text in bold, **like this**, are explained in the glossary.

Contents

Introduction

From 1978 until the end of 2001 the remote and poverty-stricken Asian country of Afghanistan was torn apart by war. Millions died or were disabled, and millions more were forced from their homes and turned into **refugees**. Most of the country's already inadequate roads, **irrigation systems**, schools and health services were destroyed. During these years of conflict and violence children sometimes learned to use a gun before they learned to read and write.

The impact of the wars in Afghanistan spread far beyond its borders. The **Soviet Union's** military intervention in Afghanistan made the Soviet government more unpopular with its own people, and was one of the causes of the break up of the Soviet Union and the collapse of **communism** throughout eastern Europe. The success of the **Islamic** resistance to the Soviet intervention gave a huge boost to **Islamic fundamentalism** across the world. Later the triumph of one particular fundamentalist group – the Taliban – turned Afghanistan into a safe haven for Islamic **terrorist** groups like al-Qaeda. The shocking success of al-Qaeda's 11 September 2001 attack on the USA has created a new and uncertain world in which some countries – most notably the USA itself – have become convinced that attack is the best form of defence.

This picture of the Bamian Valley, and the mountains that surround it, gives a good idea of Afghanistan's vast and difficult **terrain**.

Who fought who?

Civil war broke out in Afghanistan in 1978 and was mostly brought to a close in December 2001. However, this was not one long war between two sides, but a series of wars in which the warring parties changed on several occasions. The first war (1978–9) was fought between the communist government's supporters and their **conservative** Islamic opponents. This war was widened (1979–89) when the Soviet Union sent troops and weapons into the country to help the communists at the same time as the USA and Pakistan were giving **covert** support to the Islamic fighting groups known as the *mujahedin*. After the Soviets withdrew their forces the fighting continued between the communists and the *mujahedin* (1989–92). When the Afghan communists were finally defeated, the various *mujahedin* groups fought a civil war between themselves (1992–6). A new group of Islamic fundamentalists, called the Taliban, conquered most of the country between 1994 and 1998, but were in turn overthrown by the USA and its **allies** in late 2001, in the first major action of the **War on Terrorism**.

What were they fighting for?

What were these wars about? The basic conflict was between modernization and tradition. On the one side were those people who wanted to see Afghanistan turned into a modern **secular** state. On the other side were those who did not want change, who wanted religious leadership and who deeply distrusted the modern world – especially the modern **Western** world. These divisions within Afghan society became part of the much larger **Cold War**, as the Soviet Union offered military backing to the modernizers and the USA offered support to the traditionalists.

As the war lengthened, old rivalries between Afghanistan's different **ethnic groups** – Pashtun, Uzbek, Tajik and Hazara – came to the surface (see map on page 8). A war about modernization turned into a war between ethnic groups. Eventually, the Taliban gained control of most of the country and imposed a harsh and extreme form of Islamic law on the Afghan people. However, with the launch of the War on Terrorism, Afghanistan once again became the focus of a wider war, and the Taliban found itself fighting a losing battle with the USA and its allies.

How do we know?

If we want to understand something that happened in the past, where do we start? Most bookshops and libraries have shelves of history books, and there's a good chance that whatever subject we want to study, some historian will have written a book about it. This historian will have looked at different accounts of the events and tried to understand the motives of those involved. He or she will have explored the background to these events and probably tried to explain how they have affected the future.

Such books are often interesting and informative. But how accurate are they? Most will have been written many years after the events they describe, by people who can perhaps imagine, but not know exactly, what life was like in the times they are writing about. Of course, each historian also has his or her own opinions and feelings about different political or social ideas. All good historians try to get past their own opinions and feelings when dealing with their chosen subjects, but it is not an easy thing to do.

Another problem facing historians is the incompleteness of the information they have to work with. There were, for example, over a million people involved in the Battle of Stalingrad during World War II (1939–45), but only a few hundred of them left a personal record of what happened. Some of these records would have been written down at the time, for example in a soldier's diary, or a journalist's report. Other people would have written

A TV journalist speaks to the camera against the backdrop of Afghanistan's mountains. He is reporting on 'Operation Enduring Freedom', part of the **War on Terrorism**, in October 2001. Historians would consider such film footage a valuable primary source.

down their experiences after the event, and sometimes with the intention of justifying their own actions. Historians will sift through these primary sources, aware that they are only reading part of the story, and they will try to build up a wider picture of what really happened and why. Their books will then become secondary sources for future historians.

The cost of war. Two men crippled by land mines move around among the ruins of the Afghan capital city Kabul in 1996.

This book uses both an historian's account and a wide selection of primary sources to tell the story of Afghanistan since 1978. Since this is mostly a story of war, many of the primary sources tend to support one side or the other. This is true whether the source in question comes from an important national figure, like a US National Security advisor (see page 19) or simply an ordinary Afghan caught up in events, like the teacher in Kabul (see page 33). Sometimes a source is trying to make a political point, like the writer in the government newspaper (see page 11), at others he or she is simply trying to express what it felt like to be there, like the **Soviet** soldier sent to fight or the young woman forced to wear particular clothes (see pages 17 and 39). But even **biased** sources can contribute to the wider historical picture. They can reveal people's **prejudices** allowing us to understand why people act in the way they do. Many primary sources, like the ones in this book, often provide the most dramatic picture of what it was really like to live through certain times or events.

Afghanistan before 1978

Afghanistan is a country of rugged mountains and deserts in Central Asia. As a unified country, with clearly defined borders, Afghanistan only came into existence in the 19th century. Unfortunately, its political boundaries marking the provinces didn't match the tribal boundaries of the people and this has been the cause of many of its problems ever since. Also, Afghanistan lay between the British and Russian (later, **Soviet Union**) **empires**, neither of which allowed the other to rule it directly as a **colony**.

Afghanistan has few **natural resources**, which may be one reason why it was never colonized. Colonization would have provided the power and money to push through the modernization of the country's economic and social **infrastructure** – its communications, administration, education and health care. As this never happened, the country remained isolated and undeveloped well into the second half of the 20th century. By 1978 it had an estimated population of between 15 and 20 million, and most of these people scraped a poor living from farming. There were four major cities: Kabul, the capital city, in the east, Kandahar in the south, Herat in the west and Mazar-i-Sharif in the north. Afghans were divided into four large **ethnic groups** – the Pashtuns, Tajiks, Uzbeks and Hazaras – and several much smaller groups. Nearly all of these were **Muslims**. Most were from the majority **Sunni** group, but the Hazaras were mostly from the minority **Shi'a** group.

Map of Afghanistan showing the ethnic group in each area.

UZBEKISTAN TAJIKISTAN CHINA

TURKMENISTAN

IRAN

● Mazar-i-Sharif

PANJSHIR VALLEY NURISTAN

Bamiyan ●

●Herat

Kabul ● ●Jalalabad

AFGHANISTAN

N
W ⊕ E
S

0   200 km
0   200 miles

● Kandahar

PAKISTAN

Pashtun	Kyrgyz
Tajik	Turkmen
Hazara	Nuristani
Uzbek	Pamiri
Aimak	Other
Baluchi	

Sandy Gall describes an ancient land

British television reporter Sandy Gall travelled extensively in rural Afghanistan during the war between the Soviets and the **mujahedin**. In this passage from one of his books, published in 1988, he provides a vivid snapshot of life in this poor and undeveloped country.

We rode on past small fields, squeezed between the river and the mountain, protected by high, drystone walls, where only the women it seemed were at work. As we passed they would draw their veils across their faces, but not before we caught a glimpse of their features, old before their time, worn by toil and the harshness of their lives. They never spoke, never smiled, behaved almost as if we did not exist. While they worked, their babies hung under the trees, suspended in conical baskets woven from goat's hair. Only the young girls were less shy, darting surreptitious glances at us as we passed and giggling at one another.

Kabul, a city built on several hills, is pictured here a few years before the wars. It had a population of some 350,000. Compare this picture with the one on page 33.

The men were slightly friendlier, stopping to look up from whatever they were doing, returning a salutation when they passed us on the track... In clearings among the trees, or a bank above the river, stood small log cabins, idyllic in their remote tranquillity, each household virtually self-sufficient. Half-naked and usually very dirty children would come and peer at us with huge dark eyes.

The 1978 coup

For most of the 20th century Afghan politics was a contest between those who wanted to modernize the country and those who wanted to hang on to traditional ways of life. The modernizers said they wanted economic development, a more **democratic** political system, better education, more land for the poor and equal rights for women. The traditionalists thought that such policies would create a **Western-style secular** society, which ran counter to the teachings of **Islam**.

In 1978, a **dictator** named Daoud Khan ruled Afghanistan. Over the previous five years he had introduced some modernization measures, hoping to satisfy the modernizers without upsetting the traditionalists. He ended up annoying both. In the April 1978 **coup**, Daoud Khan was overthrown by the most powerful group of modernizers in Afghanistan, the **communist** 'People's Democratic Party of Afghanistan' (PDPA).

On taking power, the PDPA announced a campaign to increase **literacy** among both males and females, and to drastically reduce the interest charges, which many poor Afghans were paying on their debts. There was much support for these measures, and it was hoped that a large influx of **Soviet** aid would help boost the development of the country's economy as well as increasing the popularity of the party and its government.

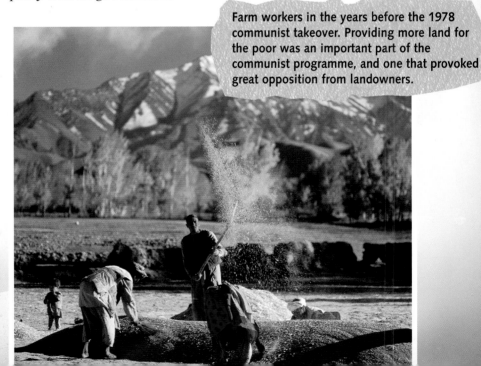

Farm workers in the years before the 1978 communist takeover. Providing more land for the poor was an important part of the communist programme, and one that provoked great opposition from landowners.

Naji Nasruddin is a happy peasant
This lengthy expression of praise for the government appeared, not surprisingly, in the government-controlled *Kabul Times* newspaper on 13 February 1979. Some **peasants** welcomed the **land reform** policy for the reasons Naji Nasruddin describes, but many opposed it. By quoting him, the newspaper was trying to paint government policy in a positive light.

THE KABUL TIMES

13 February 1979

Naji Nasruddin, a peasant from Balla Bagh village said smilingly, 'God is with those who are helpless. Consequently the Decree Number Eight [which fixed the maximum amount of land which anyone could own, and announced that the excess would be given to the landless] has come to our rescue. Hereafter whatever we reap belongs to us. Hereafter no landlords or middlemen will be able to cheat us. This has all happened because the communists are in power. We the toiling peasants have been delivered forever. Today the government is headed by those who work solely for the benefit, for the welfare, of the poor and downtrodden. Now with the land given to me I am sure I will become the owner of a decent living and will not die of hunger.'

Opposition

There was much opposition to the new government and its policies. The traditionalists claimed that these policies, and particularly those which were designed to achieve greater equality for women, were anti-**Islamic**. Self-interest played a part in this opposition as many local religious leaders were in fact also the local landlords and money-lenders. They were now receiving less interest on the money they were owed, and they also stood to lose land when the government introduced its promised **land reform**. Not surprisingly, they used their religious influence to organize political opposition to the **communists**.

Different opposing groups or parties emerged from the various **ethnic groups** in different parts of the country, each with their own fighters or *mujahedin*, all united under the banner of Islam. Some were more fervently Islamic than others. *Hezb-e-Islami*, which was led by Gulbuddin Hekmatyar (a Pashtun), was, for example, more **Islamic fundamentalist** than *Jamiat-e-Islami*, which was led by two Tajiks, Burhanuddin Rabbani and Ahmad Shah Massoud.

As the **civil war** intensified all these groups sought support from abroad. The **Cold War** between the **Soviet Union** and the **West**, which had dominated world politics since 1947, was still going on, and the leaders of the various Afghan *mujahedin* groups knew that anyone fighting communism could expect help from the West.

The domes of a simple mosque in the small town of Khulm in northern Afghanistan. Most Afghans are Muslim followers of the religion of Islam. Their holy book is the Qur'an.

A rebel addresses a meeting
In this account, an unnamed man from the Khunar region describes how he spoke at a meeting called to discuss opposition to the communist government. Just as the government newspaper report on the previous page exaggerated support for its policies, so this man exaggerates and distorts what the government is doing. **Muslims** were not being killed simply for being Muslims, but because they opposed the government's policies.

On the fifteenth of Saur 1358 (5 May 1979) a general *jirgah* of the *Mohmand* tribes was held in Gandab [across the border in Pakistan]. I participated and spoke.

After introducing myself I encouraged the people to join the **jihad** by saying that our fathers fought against the English, and that here and now in Afghanistan the Khalqis and Parchamis who are communists and atheists [people who do not believe in the existence of god] have taken power. Hundreds of Muslims have been killed for the crime of being Muslims, and nearly a year has gone by that the peoples of Kumar have been fighting the communists. We have two moral claims on you. The first is that you are Muslims and therefore obliged to wage jihad. The other is that our fathers waged jihad here with you, and you also must repay the debt to us by waging jihad shoulder to shoulder with us.

At the conclusion of the jirgah, we decided as one that we must wage jihad.

Civil war

Throughout 1978–9 the gap between the modernizing **communist** government and the traditionalist opposition groups grew steadily wider. The communists themselves were split between two groups: the dominant and extreme Khalq group led by Nur Muhammad Taraki and Hafizullah Amin, and the more moderate Parcham group under Babrak Karmal. When many in the country opposed communist policies, the Parcham group advised the government to introduce the planned changes more gradually, so that people would have a chance to get used to them. The Khalq group, however, was determined to push ahead at full speed. Instead of moderating their policies, Taraki and Amin brought forward new, more extreme proposals including **land reform** and equal rights for women.

This increased the number and anger of their traditionalist opponents. In late 1978 *mujahedin* groups in the north-eastern region of Nuristan rose in revolt, and in March 1979 fighters under the *mujahedin* leader in the west, Ismail Khan, seized control of Herat, the country's third-largest city. Several thousand people were killed before government forces retook the city.

After this tragedy, the more extreme Amin took charge. He launched a reign of terror across the country, arresting and killing anyone who dared oppose him, including many fellow-communists. In September, Taraki was killed in a palace confrontation, leaving Amin in complete control. But his brutal methods only served to further increase the numbers of those who opposed his government, both inside and outside Afghanistan. Throughout the country, **civil war** was now taking hold.

Hafizullah Amin gives a press conference on 23 September 1979, nine days after leading the **coup** which resulted in the death of fellow-communist leader Nur Muhammad Taraki.

A telephone conversation between Nur Muhammed Taraki and Soviet prime minister, Alexei Kosygin

On 18 March 1979, at the height of the Herat uprising against the communist government, **Soviet** prime minister Alexei Kosygin and Afghan prime minister Nur Muhammad Taraki spoke on the telephone. This extract from the written record of their conversation shows how reluctant the Soviets were to intervene in Afghanistan.

Kosygin: What is the situation in Herat?

Taraki: We think that either this evening or tomorrow morning Herat will fall and be in the hands of the enemy.

Kosygin: And what will happen then?

Taraki: We are sure that the enemy [the *mujahedin*] will form new units and will continue the offensive.

Kosygin: Do you have enough forces to defeat them?

Taraki: If only we had.

Kosygin: What do you suggest then?

Taraki: We ask that you send us practical and technical assistance - men and weapons.

Kosygin: This is a very complicated problem.

Taraki: Otherwise the rebels will go to Kandahar and then to Kabul. They will bring many Iranians into Afghanistan. Afghans who have fled to Pakistan will come back. Iran and Pakistan have a common plan against us. But if you come to the rescue of Herat now then the **revolution** may be saved. I ask you to help us.

Kosygin: I must talk to my colleagues about this.

Taraki: While you are talking Herat will fall, and both the Soviet Union and Afghanistan will have still greater difficulties.

Soviet intervention

The increasing intensity of the conflict now raging inside Afghanistan put the **Soviet** government in a difficult position. They wanted to help the Afghan **communists**, and were reluctant to see a successful communist **revolution** overturned in a **civil war**. Also, if the Afghan communist revolution failed this might encourage other peoples to overthrow their communist governments. Still, they were reluctant to intervene directly. As we have seen, when Taraki asked them to do so at the time of the Herat uprising in March 1979, they refused.

Amin's reckless brutality, and his killing of Taraki, probably convinced the Soviets that they would have to intervene to remove him. On 12 December 1979, at a meeting of the Soviet leadership, it was decided that military intervention was necessary to save the communist government from both its own leader and its Afghan enemies. The plan was for Soviet troops to secure the country's main cities and roads, and give the Parcham leader Babrak Karmal time to introduce a more moderate communist programme. Such a programme, the Soviets reckoned, would win over enough of the government's enemies to keep the communists in power.

In December 1979 Soviet tanks rolled across the border that separated the two countries. Amin was killed, Karmal installed in his place, and Soviet troops fanned out to occupy key positions across the country. For a few days, the intervention seemed successful. But the Soviet leadership had seriously underestimated the level of resistance to this intervention, both inside the country and abroad.

Soviet tanks arrive in snowbound Kabul, January 1980.

Igor goes to war

During two long periods in Afghanistan, Soviet journalist Artyom Borovik interviewed many of the Soviet soldiers on duty there. In this extract, Igor Koval'chuk, a twenty-year-old from Kharkov in the Ukraine, describes how he went to war and what the authorities told him he was fighting for.

After saying goodbye to my parents, my sister and my friends, I left my native and beloved city in the spring of 1980. The train took us south. We spent the time playing cards and drinking vodka. We spent twelve days like this and then found ourselves in Turkmenistan [a part of the old Soviet Union close to Afghanistan].

The hard days of basic training started. For each ten recruits there were two sergeants who taught us everything – attacking, defending, working with the bayonet and the butt of the gun, and, of course, shooting.

In two and a half months we took our **oath of allegiance**. We were all lined up and told that we were very lucky, that we had the great honour to be trusted by the [Soviet Communist] Party to fulfil our international duty in Afghanistan. We had to help the Afghan people retain the conquests of the April Revolution [the 1978 **coup**], they said, and defend them from the bloodthirsty actions of **imperialism**, which, by invading the territory of our [Afghan] **ally**, threatened our southern border.

Help for the mujahedin

The USA and their **allies** condemned the **Soviet** intervention and took steps to punish the Soviet leadership. **Nuclear disarmament** talks between the two **superpowers** were put on hold, and the USA **boycotted** the 1980 Olympics in the Soviet capital city, Moscow.

The USA was, however, already giving assistance to the **mujahedin** – President Carter had secretly authorised this in July 1979 – and this aid was now expanded. Over the next ten years the *mujahedin* would receive around $3–4 billion from the USA. This was not because the US government was pro-**Islamic**, but because it was anti-Soviet. The USA wanted to tie down the Soviet armies in an unwinnable war so as to cause maximum damage to the Soviet economy. The USA and its **allies** gave most of their aid to the more **fundamentalist** *mujahedin* groups because they thought these groups would do the most damage to their Soviet enemy.

Mujahedin **troops in eastern Afghanistan, shortly before leaving on an operation against the Soviet invaders, January 1980.**

After condemning the Soviets' open intervention, the USA was reluctant to let the world know that it too was intervening. The USA reached secret agreements with Afghanistan's neighbour Pakistan. In exchange for a huge increase in US economic aid, Pakistan's **intelligence service**, the ISI, agreed to deliver US aid to their Afghan allies.

Other **Muslim** countries – most notably, Saudi Arabia, Egypt and Iran – also gave financial assistance to their fellow Muslims in Afghanistan, and a steady stream of individuals began arriving in Afghanistan from all over the Muslim world, eager to take part in what they saw as a holy war.

Zbigniew Brzezinski makes an admission
Zbigniew Brzezinski was US National Security Adviser during the administration of President Carter. In this interview, which was given to the French magazine *Le Nouvel Observateur* in January 1998, almost twenty years after the Soviet intervention in Afghanistan, Brzezinski admits that he and Carter deliberately encouraged that intervention.

LE NOUVEL OBSERVATEUR

January 1998

Brzezinski: According to the official version of history, CIA [Central Intelligence Agency] aid to the *mujahedin* began during 1980, that is to say, after the Soviet army invaded Afghanistan, 24 Dec 1979. But the reality, secretly guarded until now, is completely otherwise. Indeed, it was July 3 1979 that President Carter signed the first directive for secret aid to the opponents of the pro-Soviet regime in Kabul. And that very day, I wrote a note to the president in which I explained to him that in my opinion this aid was going to induce a Soviet military intervention.

Interviewer: Despite this risk, you were an advocate of this **covert** action. But perhaps you yourself desired this Soviet entry into war and looked to provoke it?

Brzezinski: It isn't quite that. We didn't push the Russians to intervene, but we knowingly increased the probability that they would.

Jimmy Carter was the president of the USA at the time of the Soviet intervention. Carter and his National Security adviser, Zbigniew Brzezinski, were keen to encourage opposition to the Soviet-backed **communist** government in Afghanistan.

The military conflict

In the beginning, the **Soviet** armed forces had little trouble holding the main towns and the roads that connected them. Their problems began when they tried to take control of the rest of the country, where most of the people lived. The small villages which dotted the Afghan landscape of deep valleys and high mountains were easy enough to seize, but they were not suitable as permanent **garrisons**, and the moment the Soviet soldiers left, the **mujahedin** took them back again. Also, movement between the villages was always risky. Soviet patrols would come under fire, lose a few men, and then find that the *mujahedin* had slipped away before they had the chance to fight back. By resorting to **guerrilla tactics** the *mujahedin* made the most of their natural advantages – the difficult **terrain** and the support of the rural people. This prevented the Soviets from making the most of their advantages – complete control of the sky (the *mujahedin* had no aircraft), sophisticated communications technology and better weapons.

The Soviets grew increasingly frustrated at their inability to make any headway. They relied more and more on air attacks, which killed far more **civilians** than fighters. As feelings of hatred deepened, the number of atrocities committed by both sides rose.

Soviet casualties were relatively low during the early years of the war, but in 1986 the *mujahedin* received their first Stinger anti-aircraft missiles from the USA, and casualties rose steeply, particularly among Soviet air-crews. By this time it was clear to many people that the Afghan government and their Soviet supporters had little hope of winning the war.

A *mujahedin* **commander** gives lessons in weapon use at a training camp inside Afghanistan in 1987.

Artyom Borovik describes a successful ambush
During his work as a war correspondent in Afghanistan, Artyom Borovik witnessed many minor battles between the Soviet forces and the *mujahedin.* His editors in Moscow were no doubt more interested in Soviet successes, like the one described here, than the many failures. Still, Borovik manages to convey a feeling of what the war was like for those involved.

We let the band of rebels [*mujahedin*] draw as close as possible, our nerves near breaking point. Desperate shooting starts down below. The dark is pierced by intermittent flashes of gunfire. About a dozen rebels flee towards the right bank of the river. Several fall to the ground; five or six others drop behind boulders. A few moments later they open fire to cover the rebels who are trying to break through between us and the neighbouring hill. There's thunder on my left and right: Dzhabarov and Kirillov are firing their machine guns at three *dukhi* [the Russian word for 'ghosts', which became the Soviet soldiers' slang term for the *mujahedin*] who are trying to outflank us on the left. Then the fireworks begin. Tracer bullets cut the darkness into stripes... it looks as if someone has stretched red and yellow wires across the night sky. But soon the glowing wires fade into the blackness. There are no *dukhi* left. The battle has lasted ten minutes.

Life for Afghans in the mid-1980s

By the mid-1980s at least 50,000 Afghan soldiers, government forces and **mujahedin**, had been killed or injured, along with around 20,000 **Soviet** troops. The number of **civilians** maimed or killed by artillery shells, rockets, bombs and land-mines had not been counted, but ran into tens – perhaps hundreds – of thousands. Half the country's schools and hospitals, and well over a hundred local health clinics, had been destroyed.

Much of Afghanistan, outside of the main cities, had become a series of mini-states, run by **warlords** in the name of **Islam**. Some of these warlords, like the ruthless Hekmatyar, inspired fear rather than affection; others, like Massoud in the Panjshir Valley, were adored by their followers. These warlords set up their own administrations in the areas they controlled, administering justice, distributing the incoming aid, and trying to protect their people from outside attacks.

In the main towns it was a different matter. The government's modernization programme still had its active supporters, and there were many town-dwellers who feared **Islamic fundamentalists** like Hekmatyar more than they feared the **communists**. Those who dared oppose the government were kept in line by the KhAD **security police**, which had been modelled on the Soviet **KGB**. KhAD was led by Muhammad Najibullah, and he had a reputation for both efficiency and barbarity.

Mujahedin **commander Ahmad Shah Massoud (on the right), reading by the light of a kerosene lamp in a home in the Panjshir Valley – 1985.**

Arielle Calemjane remembers one day in the Panjshir valley

During the mid-80s, at the height of the Soviet-*mujahedin* conflict, many areas of the Afghan countryside were subjected to frequent and terrifying Soviet bombardments from the air. In this account, Arielle Calemjane, a nurse working for the French organization Aide Medicale Internationale in the Panjshir Valley, describes one day of terror in July 1984.

The helicopters and airplanes come. On the road, entire families are climbing the sides of the valley. The children in the women's arms have such big black eyes; they do not cry. The women's faces are hidden behind their veils; impossible to know what they think. The men go on foot, staring into the distance, searching for cover.

Suddenly there are bombs exploding around us – what are they aiming at? There are a few houses nearby; the people are fleeing. I am seized by an uncontrollable trembling, prey to a feeling of total powerlessness against these big black birds, these horrible black spots in the sky, these huge insects whose sound is the sound of hell and who sow destruction and death.

We are invited into a house. A wounded man is on the floor, his hand wrapped in a bandage from which blood is dripping. The helicopter fired while he was on horseback, holding a child in front of him. The bullet passed through his left hand, and killed the child. We have to amputate three fingers down to the knuckle.

The wider impact of the war in Afghanistan

Outside Afghanistan, those countries most affected by the war were Pakistan and Iran. It was these two **Muslim** countries that provided shelter for those who fled the war. By the end of the 1980s there were almost 6 million **refugees** living in makeshift camps – more than a quarter of the Afghan population. This not only placed a strain on the Pakistani and Iranian economies, but also allowed both states to strengthen their own positions in Afghanistan itself. Iran, as a **Shi'a Muslim** country, was keen to help its fellow Shi'as, and particularly the main Shi'a **ethnic group**, the Hazaras. Pakistan, which has more Pashtuns than Afghanistan, gave its main support to Hekmatyar, the leader of the dominant Pashtun group. Pakistan wanted to see a **Soviet** defeat because its main enemy, India, was **allied** to the Soviet Union.

In the Muslim world the contest between the Soviets and the *mujahedin* became a symbol of a much wider conflict between **Western** ways (**communism** was considered a Western idea) and the way of **Islam**. Many Muslims saw *mujahedin* success in the war against the Soviets as a triumph for the old ways and a sign that the long years of foreign intervention in Muslim affairs might be coming to an end. Such feelings inspired many young Muslims to volunteer for military service in Afghanistan. Osama bin Laden, the future leader of the **terrorist** group al-Qaeda, was one of them.

Adrogal Gul's life

This extract comes from an article written by M. H. Ahsan entitled 'The Forgotten Refugees' and describes the life of a single Afghan refugee in vivid and harrowing detail.

It is nearly midnight in Peshawar, a small city in northwest Pakistan, and Adrogal Gul is laying out his blanket, preparing for bed. His mattress is a slab of concrete tucked in the lee of a dumpster [large container for holding rubbish] in a filthy parking lot near the city's White Mosque. The sidewalk [pavement] is cold and his blanket is thin, perhaps mercifully so, as it is home to vermin that leave nickel-size welts. Forty or so men line the sidewalks nearby. Like Adrogal, nearly all are Afghan refugees.

Adrogal offers up a hand so swollen and calloused it resembles a small baseball glove, then he considers his plight. 'I came to Pakistan as a baby in my mother's arms,' he says. Except for two short stays in Afghanistan, he has lived all his twenty-two years in Pakistan, mostly in refugee camps and illegal settlements. Yet he has no citizenship. In fact, he has no documentation of any kind. Officially he does not exist.

A temporary camp for Afghan refugees in neighbouring Pakistan in 1988. Millions of Afghans ended up in refugee camps as a result of the conflict that was taking place in their country.

The Soviet withdrawal

Most of the **Soviet** soldiers who served in Afghanistan were conscripts – young men who were ordered by their government to fight. Since the fighting lasted nine years, tens of thousands of Soviet families were affected by the war.

In the early 1980s open protest was not allowed in the Soviet Union, but all that changed when Mikhail Gorbachev became Soviet leader in March 1985. As part of his plan for the reconstruction (*perestroika*) of the Soviet economy and society, he encouraged more openness (*glasnost*). This led, in the late 1980s, to growing criticism of the war from both the media and the general public.

Gorbachev himself was far from certain that Soviet involvement in Afghanistan was a good idea. It was making the government unpopular and it cost a great deal of money, which the country did not have. It was not even proving successful. Gorbachev tried to change things round, bringing in Najibullah to replace Karmal and telling him to win over the Afghan people with more moderate policies. In the meantime, he gave the Soviet generals two years to show that they could win the war.

Mikhail Gorbachev (on right) meets Muhammad Najibullah (on left) in Tashkent, April 1988. At this meeting Gorbachev announced that Soviet forces would start withdrawing from Afghanistan the following month.

By the end of 1987 it was obvious that both Najibullah and the generals had failed. In February 1988 Gorbachev announced that Soviet forces would soon be withdrawn from Afghanistan. A year later they were gone.

Mikhail Gorbachev explains why it happened

This extract is taken from the so-called 'Crimean Article', which Mikhail Gorbachev wrote in August 1991, a few days before the attempted military **coup**, which triggered the final break-up of the Soviet Union. By this time, Gorbachev felt free to express his feelings about the Afghan conflict.

The Soviet Union really did make desperate efforts to play the part of a '**superpower**', but it succeeded in doing so only in one respect – the military. Our prestige was the prestige of military force. Soviet troops were stationed in eastern Europe and Mongolia; our young men were dying in Afghanistan. At the same time the excessive military machine that had been created undermined our economy and condemned the non-military branches of the economy to appalling stagnation. The standard of living declined. In the end we could have found ourselves faced with the choice: either to bring the whole world into our gunsights or agree to fall behind in the military sense.

So we put an end to the foreign policy that served the unrealistic aim of spreading **communist** ideas round the world, that had led us into the dead end of the **Cold War**, inflicted on the people an intolerable burden of military expenditure, and dragged us into adventures like the one in Afghanistan.

Najibullah

The **Soviet Union** pulled their troops out of Afghanistan, but Soviet advisers remained with the Afghan government's army, and Soviet planes delivered the military and food supplies which the Najibullah government needed to survive. US assistance to the ***mujahedin***, far from ending, was actually increased by the new administration of George Bush Snr. in 1989. The *mujahedin*, who had not been consulted during the negotiations that accompanied the Soviet withdrawal, just kept on fighting.

Najibullah and the Soviet government hoped that eventually the country would tire of war, and that the **communist** PDPA could join, or lead, a new **coalition government**, which would include at least some of the *mujahedin* parties. In the meantime, the Najibullah government tried to make itself more acceptable to traditionally-minded Afghans. It abandoned communist policies like **collective ownership** and equal rights for women, and argued that it too was following the way of **Islam**. Few were convinced.

Despite this, the Najibullah government survived for another three years. The steady supply of Soviet arms and food helped, and so did Soviet money, which was used to buy the support of local **warlords**. The main reason for Najibullah's survival, though, was the chronic disunity of his *mujahedin* enemies, who often seemed more interested in fighting each other than in fighting the government.

KABUL NEW TIMES

23 November 1986

In the course of this year we have changed. The Party [the PDPA] and the people have changed. Everyone remembers the 16th plenum [a PDPA conference held in late 1985] and the decisions that were taken to widen the support for the **revolution**. Stress was laid on the need to win new political **allies**, from all different levels of society, and to involve them in running the country. We said that we were ready to make concessions to small businessmen and some landlords if that would help bring the fighting to an end. We agreed to take account of historic customs, traditions and national characteristics. I can say that the PDPA is the only organized force that is fully aware of the needs of the people, and the only force that struggles for their interests, leads revolutionary changes and puts into effect a policy of national reconciliation [restoring friendly relations].

Soviet soldiers wait for their former *mujahedin* enemies to collect a **UN** shipment of food aid at the Soviet-Afghan border in 1990.

Mujahedin disunity

Soon after the departure of the last **Soviet** troops in February 1989, a large *mujahedin* force laid siege to the important eastern town of Jalalabad. Contrary to expectations, they failed to take it. Communications between the *mujahedin* groups involved were poor, and other groups had not been consulted about the operation. After the failure they all blamed each other.

Mujahedin **troops fire a 122mm cannon during their unsuccessful siege of Jalalabad in March 1989.**

In the past there had been several attempts to bring these groups together. Some had looked successful: in 1985, for example, the seven main parties had established an alliance, and in February 1989 this body had elected an **interim government** to rule Afghanistan after the expected *mujahedin* victory. But behind this appearance of unity was fierce rivalry between the **ethnic groups**, each with their own ideal of **Islamic** government.

The Soviet Union finally broke up at the end of 1991, and aid to the Najibullah government ceased. In April 1992 that government finally collapsed. The *mujahedin* interim government took over, but relations between the groups swiftly degenerated into open conflict. Over the following four years four major groups tried to gain control of Kabul: the *Hezb-e-Islami*, made up mainly of Pashtuns, was led by **warlord** Hekmatyar; the *Jamiat-e-Islami*, made up mostly of Tajiks, was led by warlords Rabbani and Massoud; the Uzbek **militia** led by Dostum; and the Wahadat militia, recruited from Hazara **refugees** in Kabul, led by Abdul Ali Mazari. These groups fought battle after battle for parts of the capital, reducing much of it to ruins.

Ahmad Shah Massoud speaks to television reporters

In this account, given to the US television company CNN in 2001, Ahmad Shah Massoud, the Tajik warlord, expresses the bitterness he felt towards rival Pashtun *mujahedin* commander Gulbuddin Hekmatyar. Other *mujahedin* commanders felt much the same, but Hekmatyar disputed their version of events. Part of the historian's job is to weigh the evidence in support of conflicting statements.

Pakistan wanted someone who could just fulfil and implement the Pakistani's interests in Afghanistan. That was Hekmatyar. The modern weapons at first were sent to Hekmatyar's commanders, and it was Hekmatyar who was able to use these weapons. Hekmatyar first got the Stinger missiles, and his commanders received modern artillery. It was a **unilateral** distribution of arms, and Hekmatyar also wanted to exterminate other parties and other people so as to avoid problems in the future. They [the Pakistanis] also wanted to fan the internal fighting, and Hekmatyar thought that he would exterminate all his rivals. They were very optimistic, and they encouraged Hekmatyar by giving him arms and ammunition. Hekmatyar himself announced, after the collapse of the **communist** regime, that 'I have ammunition and arms to fight on for fifteen years,' and he was able to continue the fighting after the collapse of the regime.

Pakistani and Saudi Arabian government ministers (seated on far left and far right) persuade Ahmad Shah Massoud (second from left) and Gulbuddin Hekmatyar (second from right) to stop the fighting between their two *mujahedin* factions, 26 May 1992. The agreement was short-lived.

31

A country in ruins

By the mid-1990s Afghanistan had become a prime example of what some people call a 'failed state'. There was no single authority responsible for administering the laws and looking after the well-being of the people; even the capital city, Kabul, was divided between different **warlords**. The *mujahedin* groups had always been divided by mistrust, resentment and even hatred, but while there were **Soviet** troops inside Afghanistan they concealed these differences in order to defeat the common enemy. Now, that common enemy had gone. Afghanistan had traditionally been ruled by the Pashtuns, but the Tajiks, Uzbeks and Hazaras had fought just as long and hard against the Soviet army, and they were no longer willing to accept Pashtun domination, particularly when the most influential Pashtun leader was the much-hated Hekmatyar.

The fighting was now mostly in the cities as the different *mujahedin* groups sought to fill the vacuum left by the **communist** government, a reversal of the situation in the 1980s – but almost twenty years of war had left a terrible mark on the whole country. Over a million people had died, and a million and a half had been left disabled. Millions more had been traumatised by violence, forced into exile, or both. Sixty per cent of schools had no buildings, and agricultural production was down to a third of what it had been in 1978. The only booming industry was drugs, because opium poppies were the easiest crop to grow on farms that had had their **irrigation systems** destroyed. The country was crying out for peace and reconstruction, but the *mujahedin* seemed trapped in their mutual hatreds.

The cultivation of opium poppies in an Afghan valley. In the 1980s and 1990s a large proportion of the heroin reaching Europe originated in Afghanistan.

One of Kabul's main streets, pictured here in 1995, after three years of in-fighting between the various *mujahedin* factions.

A teacher's account of life in Kabul

Between 1992 and 1996 there was frequent fighting between the armies of the various **warlords** in Kabul. In this account of one incident, a teacher offers a terrifying insight into what life was like for the capital's inhabitants during those years.

Fierce fighting broke out and we were all running away in the streets of Kabul. As we were running, I saw an old man who told us not to go through one of the lanes because Dostum's guards were there. He warned us that the guards would take away our children. He showed us another alley to go through which we did. We were running away with a baby in my arm, with five girls and two boys of between 18 months and 18 years old. My mother-in-law, who is an old lady, had to run with us too. People were moving as fast as they could. We reached Waselabad area and two rockets were fired towards us as we were running away. We could not tell who fired them; it could have been Dostum's or Shura-e-Nezar's or Hekmatyar's forces. We managed to find a vehicle to take us outside Kabul.

The rise of the Taliban

The group that came to dominate Afghanistan first appeared in the early 1990s. Initially, the Taliban were mostly religious students – 'talib' is Arabic for student – from *madrasahs* (**Islamic** colleges) in Pakistan. A majority of the Taliban – like their leader, **Mullah** Omar – were Afghan Pashtuns, but a large minority were Pakistanis, and there was also a significant number of Arabs. All were **Sunni Muslims** and all were militant **Islamic fundamentalists**.

The Pakistani government decided that the Taliban were now a better bet than their former **ally**, the discredited Hekmatyar. They supplied the Taliban with training facilities, food, arms, fuel and even air support. There were two main reasons for this. With a hostile India on its eastern border, Pakistan needed a friend on its western border. In addition Pakistan wanted to develop its overland trade links with the newly independent, ex-**Soviet** republics of Central Asia, something it could only do if Afghanistan was at peace. The USA also hoped that the Taliban would create the strong, central government it thought Afghanistan needed.

It took the Taliban several years to conquer most of the country. Kandahar was taken in 1994, Herat in 1995, and Kabul – after several failures – in September 1996. Once Kabul had fallen, the defeated Tajik, Uzbek and Hazara *mujahedin* groups joined together as the 'National Islamic United Front for the Salvation of Afghanistan', which became known as the Northern Alliance. But they could not prevent the Taliban from conquering most of central and northern Afghanistan by the end of 1998.

Taliban troops in Charasyab, a few kilometres south of Kabul, in February 1995. It took them another eighteen months before they occupied the capital.

Record of a conversation about the war

In this slice of conversation overheard by the author Siba Shakib, one young woman talks of what the war has cost her family, and the owner of a café expresses the bitterness which many Afghans felt towards the *mujahedin* commanders for their failure to unite against the Taliban.

'My father fought in the mountains,' says Shirin-Gol. 'Now he just sits in a corner, as helpless as my little daughter. My brother stood on a mine and lost his leg. His leg, his hand, and his child that he was leading by the hand. My other brother is a *shahid* [someone killed in a holy war], and we have buried him. I do not know if the rest of my brothers and sisters are alive.'

'If I met the leaders of the *mujahedin*,' the café owner says, 'I would ask why they went on fighting after they had driven out the Russians. Why they left Kabul in ruins. And I would say to them that I rue and regret every day I helped them. And I would ask them, what right do you have to stay in power? And I would say to them that the Taliban came to power for one reason alone. Simply because they, the *mujahedin*, went on fighting.'

A teacher in Kabul in 1996 warns children of the dangers they face from land-mines and unexploded shells.

Life under the Taliban

The Taliban were **Islamic fundamentalists**. Like all Islamic fundamentalists, they believed in strictly following the rules of **Islam**. They were determined to get rid of modern ideas and practices, which they believed ran counter to the teachings of their holy book, the Qur'an. (Most **Muslims** in the wider world did not accept the views of the Taliban.) To achieve this, they applied traditional Islamic law, or the **Sharia**, with extraordinary strictness, and added new rules to cover issues which had arisen since the original Islamic laws had been laid down.

Members of the Taliban feed movie film on to a bonfire outside a Kabul cinema, shortly after taking over the capital city in September 1996.

In order to enforce all these laws and regulations, the Taliban created a religious police, the 'Department for the Promotion of Virtue and Suppression of Vice'. Severe punishments were handed out to those caught disobeying them. Public amputations, and executions by stoning, shooting or hanging, became daily occurrences in the major cities.

Afghan arts and media were also affected by the Taliban. Television broadcasts were stopped and TV sets destroyed. Radios were allowed, but only prayers and Taliban **propaganda** were heard. Music and kite-flying – a traditional favourite with Afghan children – were both banned. Then, once the culture of the present had been destroyed, the Taliban turned to the culture of the past. They believed that images of people were forbidden under this strict Islamic law and so smashed their way through the Kabul Museum, and then dynamited the world-famous giant stone Buddhas at Bamiyan.

The Taliban broadcast their list of regulations
This is a list of regulations issued by the Taliban in the days
following their conquest of Kabul in September 1996.
They were broadcast to the capital's inhabitants on the
newly re-named Radio Sharia.

- Girls and women are not allowed to work outside the home.
- Public transport will be segregated, with a bus for women and a bus for men.
- Men must grow their beards and cut their moustaches.
- Suits and ties are forbidden. Traditional Afghani dress must be worn.
- Women and girls must wear the *burqa* [a garment covering the entire body].
- Nail polish, lipstick and make-up are forbidden.
- Displaying photos of animals or humans is forbidden.
- No male doctor is permitted to touch the body of a woman under the pretext of a consultation.
- A woman must not go to a men's tailor.
- A young woman must not engage in conversation with a young man. If they do so, they must be married immediately.
- Muslim families may not listen to music, even during a wedding ceremony.
- Families are prohibited from taking photos or making videos, even during a wedding.
- It is forbidden for non-Muslim names to be given to babies.
- All non-Muslims, that is Hindus and Jews, must wear yellow garments or some yellow cloth. Their houses must bear a yellow flag.
- No merchant is permitted to sell women's undergarments.
- When the police are punishing an offender, no one has the right to question or criticise their actions.
- All offenders against the decrees of the Sharia Law will be punished on the public square.

A woman's place

It was the Afghan women of the cities who suffered most from the Taliban's regulations. Over the previous 50 years their freedom to receive an education, to work where they wanted and to dress how they liked – had been slowly expanding. Now, suddenly, they were more oppressed than they had ever been. Women were forbidden an education, forbidden to work and forbidden to travel anywhere without a male relative. They were forced to wear the traditional *burqa*, a gown which covered them up from head to toe. In addition to all this, hundreds of young girls were forced into marriage with members of the Taliban.

Latifa writes about wearing a *burqa*
This conversation is taken from a book written by a young Afghan woman named Latifa and published in the West in 2002. The fact that she was able to write a book and have it published suggests that Latifa was probably from an educated middle-class Afghan family, and therefore not typical of most young Afghan women.

The Taliban's treatment of women caused anger throughout the world, and particularly in the **West** where women had long taken such freedoms for granted. US approval of the regime quickly turned to distaste, leaving Pakistan as the Taliban's only real **ally**. As long as the Taliban restricted its activities and influence to Afghanistan they had no need of other friends. It was only when they allowed wanted international **terrorists** to live, train and plan new operations on Afghan soil that the rest of world began to see the Taliban as an active enemy.

A Taliban soldier interrupts a class in a private girls' school in 1997. State girls' schools had already been closed, and private ones would soon suffer the same fate.

A group of Afghan women wearing *burqas*, the complete body-covering garment which was made compulsory during the time of Taliban rule.

I look at this garment, its woven cloth flowing all the way down to the ground from a closely fitted bonnet which completely covers the head. 'Try it on' Farida says, 'if you want to go out one day you'll need to be completely covered.'

I do what she asks in order to please her, but also to see what it feels like being in there. It's suffocating.

'So? Can you see me?' Farida asks.

I see her as long as I stand directly in front of her. In order to turn my head, I have to keep some of the cloth clutched beneath my chin so that the eye holes stay in place. In order to look behind me, I have to turn round completely. I can feel the rustle of my own breath inside the garment. I'm hot. My feet get tangled up in the material. I'll never be able to wear this. This is not a garment. It's a moving prison.

I climb out of the *burqa* feeling humiliated and furious. My face belongs to me. The Qur'an says that a woman can be veiled, but that she must remain recognisable. The Taliban want to steal my face, forbid us all our faces. I won't allow it. I won't give in. I won't go out with Farida.

A sanctuary for terrorists

Osama bin Laden had spent time in Pakistan and Afghanistan during the 1980s, helping to channel Arab funds and volunteers to the *mujahedin*. During this time he started up an organization called al-Qaeda, which he intended to use for worldwide military and **terrorist** operations. In 1990 he returned to Saudi Arabia, and then spent four years in Sudan building up al-Qaeda. His activities were noticed by **Western intelligence services** and the Sudanese government were asked to throw him out. Before they could do so, bin Laden left of his own accord, arriving back in Afghanistan in the spring of 1996, just as the Taliban were making their preparations for the capture of Kabul. He gave a public pledge of allegiance to **Mullah** Omar as the 'Commander of the Faithful' and promised the Taliban both financial and military help. In return, they offered him **sanctuary** in their country.

It is not known whether bin Laden kept the Taliban informed about his worldwide operations. In 1998 al-Qaeda planted bombs close to US embassies in two African countries, and in retaliation President Clinton ordered the launching of cruise missiles against suspected training camps in Afghanistan. When the Taliban refused to hand over bin Laden, the USA imposed **economic sanctions** against the regime. In October 1999 the **United Nations Security Council** repeated the US demand and added further sanctions. By allowing bin Laden to run al-Qaeda from inside Afghanistan the Taliban had turned themselves into international outcasts.

A November 2001 photograph of Osama bin Laden (on left) and Ayman al-Zawahiri, leader and deputy-leader of the al-Qaeda terrorist organization.

The voice of the United Nations
This is an excerpt from Security Council resolution 1333, adopted on 19 December 2000. As is clear from the wording, this resolution repeated the main demands of earlier resolution 1267, adopted on 15 October 1999. The Taliban government angrily rejected this resolution, as they had the last.

The Security Council, acting under Chapter VII of the Charter of the United Nations,

1. Demands that the Taliban comply with Resolution 1267 (1999) and, in particular, cease the provision of sanctuary and training for international terrorists and their organizations, take appropriate effective measures to ensure that the territory under its control is not used for terrorist installations and camps, or for the preparation or organization of terrorist acts against other States or their citizens, and cooperate with international efforts to bring indicted [accused of serious crimes] terrorists to justice.

2. Demands also that the Taliban comply without further delay with the demand of the Security Council in provision 2 of resolution 1267 (1999) that requires the Taliban to turn over Osama bin Laden to appropriate authorities in a country where he has been indicted, or to appropriate authorities in a country where he will be arrested and effectively brought to justice.

September 11

On 11 September 2001 a devastating **terrorist** attack took place in the USA. **Hijackers** seized control of four passenger airliners and flew two of them into the two towers of the New York World Trade Centre, killing almost 3000 people. The third plane was crashed into the Pentagon headquarters of the US Defense Department just outside Washington DC; the fourth crashed in Pennsylvania.

The **United Nations Security Council** condemned both the attackers and 'those responsible for aiding, supporting or harbouring the perpetrators, organizers and sponsors of these acts.' Osama bin Laden initially denied responsibility, but four days after the attack President George W. Bush announced that he was the prime suspect and demanded that his Taliban hosts hand him over. Failure to do so, Bush suggested, would trigger a US invasion of Afghanistan. The USA also put pressure on Pakistan to abandon its support for the Taliban.

The Taliban demanded proof that bin Laden had organized the attacks, and when none was offered they refused to surrender him. Though no Afghans were directly involved in the attacks, Afghanistan became the target of the USA because the Taliban decided to shield bin Laden. The Taliban may also have believed that the USA, like the **Soviet Union**, would never successfully invade Afghanistan. They were mistaken.

An airliner piloted by an al-Qaeda terrorist explodes on impact with the south tower of the World Trade Centre, 11 September 2001. The north tower has already been hit by another plane. Nearly 3000 people were killed.

George Bush issues an ultimatum

Nine days after the terrorist attack on New York and Washington DC, President George W. Bush gave a speech to Congress. In this extract he threatens the Taliban regime in Afghanistan, while trying to make it clear that his government and country has no quarrel with the Afghan people.

On September the 11th, enemies of freedom committed an act of war against our country. The evidence we have gathered all points to a collection of loosely affiliated organizations known as al-Qaeda. Al-Qaeda and its leader have great influence in Afghanistan, and support the Taliban regime in controlling most of that country.

The United States respects the people of Afghanistan – after all, we are currently its largest source of humanitarian aid – but we condemn the Taliban regime. It is not only repressing its own people, it is threatening people everywhere by sponsoring and sheltering and supplying terrorists. By aiding and abetting murder, the Taliban regime is committing murder.

And tonight the United States of America makes the following demands on the Taliban: Deliver to United States authorities all the leaders of al-Qaeda who hide in your land. Close immediately and permanently every terrorist training camp in Afghanistan, and hand over every terrorist. Give the United States full access to terrorist training camps, so we can make sure they are no longer operating.

These demands are not open to negotiation or discussion. The Taliban must act, and act immediately. They will hand over the terrorists, or they will share in their fate.

President George W. Bush addresses Congress on 20 September 2001. This was the speech in which he demanded that the Taliban hand over Osama bin Laden or face the consequences.

'Operation Enduring Freedom'

On 7 October 2001, US and British forces launched 'Operation Enduring Freedom', against Taliban-controlled Afghanistan, with a cruise missile attack. The USA had no intention of risking high American casualties in a ground war with the Taliban, preferring to use their formidable airpower to bomb the enemy into surrendering. Most of the ground fighting would be done by the USA's new **allies** – the Northern Alliance of Tajiks, Hazaras and Uzbeks, which on 11 September had controlled only a small area of north-eastern Afghanistan.

The strategy worked. Once the US had destroyed the Taliban's air defences with missiles and night bombing raids they began a relentless pounding of the Taliban's army. After three weeks of such punishment, the weakened Taliban proved no match for the Northern Alliance. Mazar-i-Sharif fell on 9 November and Kabul four days later. Kandahar would not fall for another month, but the Taliban government had been overthrown. The **warlords** of the Northern Alliance – the same men who had reduced much of Kabul to rubble in the mid-1990s – were back in the capital.

The war was won, but neither Osama bin Laden nor the Taliban leader **Mullah** Omar had been captured. Many Taliban had been killed, but others had simply melted back into the general population. Few Afghans mourned the passing of the Taliban, but the USA was not much more popular. Several thousand Afghan **civilians** had also been killed by the bombings, and many ordinary Afghans shared the belief, widespread in the **Muslim** world, that the USA was an enemy of **Islam**.

Victorious Northern Alliance fighters enter the Afghan capital city on 13 November 2001.

Mohammed Gul's account of the war

Mohammed Gul worked in a Kandahar hospital during 'Operation Enduring Freedom'. His account of the US bombing of the city paints a dramatic picture of the cost to ordinary people. Such accounts are bound to be critical, and historians will try to balance them by explaining why others considered such bombing to be necessary.

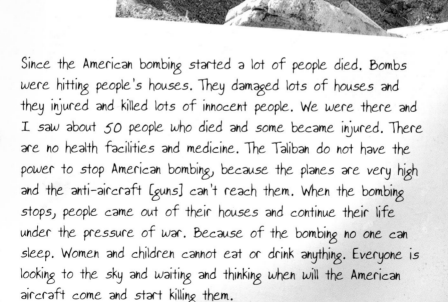

A large crater in a Kabul street, blown out by a US bomb during 'Operation Enduring Freedom'. One child was killed and four others were wounded.

Since the American bombing started a lot of people died. Bombs were hitting people's houses. They damaged lots of houses and they injured and killed lots of innocent people. We were there and I saw about 50 people who died and some became injured. There are no health facilities and medicine. The Taliban do not have the power to stop American bombing, because the planes are very high and the anti-aircraft [guns] can't reach them. When the bombing stops, people came out of their houses and continue their life under the pressure of war. Because of the bombing no one can sleep. Women and children cannot eat or drink anything. Everyone is looking to the sky and waiting and thinking when will the American aircraft come and start killing them.

A new government

Who would rule Afghanistan now that the Taliban had been overthrown? In late November the **United Nations** invited leaders from most of the Afghan parties to the city of Bonn, in Germany, for a conference to answer this question. The most notable absentees were Ahmad Shah Massoud, the Tajik **warlord**, who had been **assassinated** by al-Qaeda **suicide bombers** two days before 11 September, and Gulbuddin Hekmatyar, the Pashtun warlord, whose past behaviour had made him unacceptable to everyone else.

In Bonn an **interim government** was chosen. Its composition reflected the size of the various **ethnic groups**: the Pashtuns were given 11 seats, the Tajiks 8, the Hazaras 5, the Uzbeks 3 and others 3. Three women were also included. The chosen chairman was Hamid Karzai, a Pashtun from one of the more moderate **Islamic** parties with wide international experience.

This interim government took office in Kabul on 22 December 2001, and began the long task of organizing the political, economic and social reconstruction that the country so badly needed. For the moment, most of the country remained outside its control. US and British forces were still searching for surviving Taliban and al-Qaeda troops, and the warlords in the various regions showed no sign of surrendering their weapons or power. The United Nations organized a small international force to keep the peace in Kabul, but attempts to create similar forces for the other major cities were frustrated by US and French opposition. The international community, it seemed, was unwilling to offer the costly and whole-hearted commitment that was essential if Afghanistan was to become a peaceful and stable country.

Uzbek warlord Abdul Rashid Dostum (on left) and Hamid Karzai, then chairman of the new interim government, outside the presidential palace in Kabul, December 2001.

Around 600 fighters were captured by US forces and imprisoned as 'enemy combatants' at Guantanamo Bay, Cuba. Because these people have not been treated as prisoners of war this has become a highly controversial issue.

Hamid Karzai speaks about rebuilding Afghanistan

This extract was taken from an interview given by the new Afghan leader, Hamid Karzai, on US television in 2002.

Jim Lehrer (US broadcaster): You mentioned the destruction that has happened in your country. Tom Friedman of the *New York Times* was on our program recently, and he compared rebuilding Afghanistan to building something on the Moon. How would you describe the task of making your country a nation again? How long is it going to take?

Hamid Karzai: How long is it going to take? We will not stop, and if we stop, we will be bringing back these bad people to Afghanistan. And if you help us, the United States of America and other major countries, we will do the physical part of the country very well, very soon - reconstruct roads, reconstruct schools, reconstruct hospitals and all that, but politically we must continue forward to stabilize the country, to make it stand back on its own feet as a nation state, to make it have a defence force, to make it have a police force, to make it have institutions, to make it collect its own revenues so it begins to raise its own funds, its own money.

Prospects

What are the prospects for Afghanistan? It needs peace, and a government with authority over the whole country. It needs reconstruction of its **infrastructure** and its whole economy. But it will only get these things if both Afghans and the international community play their part.

Afghanistan's new leaders must set an example of working together. They must show their own people and the world that they have the interests of the whole country at heart, not just the interests of their own **ethnic group**. Those who want a **secular** modern Afghanistan and those who want a traditional **Islamic** Afghanistan will have to accept a compromise between the two. Guns have failed to settle the matter and have reduced their country to ruins.

An Afghan woman teaches a class of girls at a re-opened school in post-Taliban Afghanistan, March 2002.

None of this will be easy and it will be all but impossible without enormous help from the richer parts of the world. In 2002 the World Bank estimated that around $10 billion of foreign aid, spread over five years, was the minimum needed to reconstruct the war-shattered country. A year after the fall of the Taliban, only half that figure had been pledged. Some progress has been made – large numbers of girls are being educated, many women are working as doctors, a few **refugees** have returned, but there is still a terrible shortage of well-equipped schools and hospitals, decent roads and working electricity generators. If the Afghan people are not offered such aid and the hope of a better future, then the Afghan government, and the country as a whole, will probably descend once more into warring chaos.

Phil Reeves reports from Afghanistan
This quote is an extract from an article that appeared in the British newspaper *The Independent* on 24 February 2003. Under the headline 'Living in poverty and fear of abandonment, the barely functioning state that trusted its saviours', the British journalist Phil Reeves expresses the widespread fear in Afghanistan that the country is once again being ignored by the international community.

THE INDEPENDENT

24 February 2003

There is a deep concern in Kabul that the international community is losing interest even though the task of repairing the wreckage of war – let alone the even more massive job of **nation-building** – has barely begun. People remember [British Prime Minister] Tony Blair's pronouncement that the world 'will not walk away from Afghanistan, as it has done so many times before.' But Afghans have also listened with astonishment as Americans portray their country's experience since the overthrow of the Taliban as a 'success.' Now the attention of the world's media has swivelled to the deserts and oilfields of Iraq [a reference to the 2003 US and British war in Iraq]. Few in Kabul seem convinced by the repeated assurances – from the US government and its military, from the **United Nations** and Britain – that they will not be forgotten, or allowed to lapse back into bloodshed. Afghanistan is awash with hundreds of thousands of weapons, and most of them are in the hands of rival **warlords**. Though several have taken senior jobs and most have expressed verbal support for the Karzai government, they have yet to relinquish their private armies.

What have we learnt from Afghanistan?

After the overthrow of the Taliban and the creation of a new government, which included members of all the major **ethnic groups**, Afghanistan entered a period of relative peace. However, it is too soon to tell whether the peace will last.

Some lessons should have been learnt from all the years of conflict. Afghanistan's political, military and religious leaders know where a refusal to compromise can lead them. The **communists**, the *mujahedin* groups, and the Taliban – all of them insisted, at one time or another, that theirs was the only way. Their refusal to compromise cost more than a million Afghans their lives.

A French Army doctor, part of the continuing Western presence in Afghanistan, examines a young Afghan girl.

The international community has learnt two contradictory lessons from Afghanistan's tragedy. On the one hand it has learnt that foreign intervention in a **civil war** is risky, costly and likely to end badly for all sides. On the other hand, it has also learnt that turning its back on Afghanistan, as it did after the **Cold War** ended, could be just as dangerous. The rise of the Taliban, and their creation of a **sanctuary** for international **terrorists**, were the price the world paid for abandoning Afghanistan.

Perhaps the main lesson that Afghanistan has taught us is that giving people economic development, education and health care improves their lives, while giving them guns simply makes it easier for them to kill each other.

Shahmurat's story

The US journalist Jon Lee Anderson interviewed a village headman named Shahmurat. This Afghan had fought against the **communists** and their **Soviet allies** for five years, and then gave up fighting because he had come to the conclusion that all sides in the war were simply fighting for their own interests.

After five years, I realized that this war was meaningless to me, that East and **West** were both involved in Afghanistan for their own designs. These armed organizations [the communist government forces, mujahedin and Taliban] have been supported by foreign countries who don't care whether Afghans are educated or not, and they have pushed the fighting men to kill the educated people and those with culture. And so now there are no educated, cultured people anymore. The gun now governs Afghanistan. In other countries the security of the people and the property of the nation is guaranteed, and this is also so within **Islam**. But here these things have been destroyed. How can we change this? Perhaps, through the **United Nations**, enlightened people can come to power in Afghanistan. When a person is thirsty, he wants water. Afghans are thirsty for unity and peace. We are sick of war.

Young children playing on a wrecked bus in west Kabul, March 2003. Though the war has ended much still remains to be done. Despite promises from wealthier Western countries to rebuild Afghanistan most of west Kabul is still without electricity.

Timeline

1978	April	**Communists** seize power
	summer	Resistance to communist government begins
1979	March	Uprising in Herat
	September	Amin takes over as sole communist leader
	December	**Soviet** military intervention begins; Amin killed; replaced by Karmal
1980	January	Many Afghans leave their country, becoming **refugees**. Growing resistance to the Soviet occupation.
		USA officially agrees to fund resistance to Soviet intervention
1981	November	*Mujahedin* groups join together to form the 'Islamic Unity of Afghan Mujahedin' (IUAM)
1982	February	IUAM breaks up
1984	February	War intensifies
1985	March	Mikhail Gorbachev takes over as leader of the Soviet Union
1986	April	USA agrees to provide the *mujahedin* with Stinger missiles
	May	Karmal replaced by Najibullah as Afghan government leader
	July	First withdrawals of Soviet troops announced
	December	Najibullah launches 'National Reconciliation' policy
1988	February	Gorbachev announces withdrawals of all Soviet troops within a year
	June	*Mujahedin* groups form Afghan **Interim Government** in Pakistan
1989	February	Soviet withdrawal completed
	March	*Mujahedin* fail in bid to capture Jalalabad
	July	Major clashes between forces of Hekmatyar and Massoud
1991	December	Collapse of Soviet Union, end of Soviet aid to Najibullah
1992	April	Final collapse of communist government in Afghanistan, serious fighting begins between various *mujahedin* groups
1993-94		Struggle for control of Kabul
1994	November	Taliban take Kandahar
1995		Taliban take Herat, but twice driven back from Kabul
1996	spring	Osama bin Laden returns to Afghanistan
	September	Taliban capture Kabul
1997	May	Taliban capture most of the north
1998	Aug	Bombing of US embassies in Nairobi and Dar es Salaam. USA attacks al-Qaeda bases in Afghanistan.
2000	Dec	**United Nations** Resolution 1333 repeats demand that the Taliban give up Osama bin Laden
2001	9 September	Massoud **assassinated** by al-Qaeda **suicide bombers**
	11 September	Al-Qaeda attacks on New York City and the Pentagon; bin Laden named as prime suspect
	7 October	'Operation Enduring Freedom' begins in Afghanistan
	13 November	Kabul abandoned by Taliban
	December	Afghan opposition groups meet in Bonn to choose provisional government
2002	June	Hamid Karzai becomes president of Afghanistan

Find out more

Books & websites

The Cold War, David Taylor, (Heinemann, 2001)
September 11, 2001: Terrorists attack the USA, Patrick Lalley, (Heinemann, 2003)
Troubled World: The War on Terrorism, David Downing, (Heinemann, 2003)

Go exploring! Log onto Heinemann's online history resource at
http://www.heinemannexplore.co.uk

http://www.afghan-web.com
Contains a wealth of information about all aspects of Afghanistan.

http://www.guardian.co.uk/afghanistan/
A guide to issues surrounding recent events in Afghanistan.

List of primary sources

The author and publisher gratefully acknowledge the following publications
and websites from which written sources in the book are drawn. In some
cases the wording or sentence structure has been simplified to make the
material more appropriate for a school readership.

p 9   Sandy Gall: *Afghanistan: Agony of a Nation* (Bodley Head, 1988)
p 11 *Kabul Times*, 13 February 1979
p 13 David Busby Edwards: 'Origins of the anti-Soviet Jihad' in Grant M. Farr and John G. Merriam (ed): *The Afghan Resistance: The Politics of Survival* (Westview Press, 1987)
p 15 M. Hassan Kakar: *Afghanistan* (University of California Press, 1995)
p 17 Artyom Borovik: *The Hidden War: A Russian Journalist's Account of the Soviet War in Afghanistan* (Faber and Faber, 1991)
p 19 http://www.globalresearch.ca/articles/BRZ110A.html
p 21 Artyom Borovik: *The Hidden War: A Russian Journalist's Account of the Soviet War in Afghanistan* (Faber and Faber, 1991)
p 23 Jeri Laber, Barnett R. Rubin: '*A Nation is Dying*' (Northwestern University Press, 1988)
p 25 Adrogal Gul: http://www.dhamakanews.net/archives/refugees.htm
p 27 Mikhail Gorbachev: *The August Coup* (HarperCollins, 1991)
p 29 Muhammad Najibullah: *Kabul New Times*, 23 November 1986
p 31 Ahmad Shah Massoud: http://www.cnn.com/SPECIALS/2001/trade.center/massoud.html
p 33 http://www.amnesty.org/ailib/intcam/afgan/afg4.htm
p 35 Siba Shakib: *Afghanistan, where God only comes to weep* (Century, 2002)
p 37 Latifa: *My forbidden face* (Virago, 2002)
p 39 Latifa: *My forbidden face* (Virago, 2002)
p 41 http://www.ciaonet.org/cbr/cbroo/video/cbr_ctd/cbr_ctd_05.html
p 43 George Weld: http://www.likeanorb.com/wtc/
p 45 Mohammed Gul: http://www.cursor.org/stories/civilian-deaths.htm
p 47 Hamid Karzai: http://www.usatoday.com/news/world/2002/06/28/karzai-usat.htm
p 49 Phil Reeves: *The Independent*, 24 February 2003
p 51 Jon Lee Anderson: *The Lion's Grave: Dispatches from Afghanistan* (Atlantic, 2002)

Glossary

allies people, political parties or countries that support and help one another

assassinate kill someone deliberately, usually for political reasons

bias personal opinion or prejudice that affects judgement

boycott refuse to have anything to do with something, usually as a form of protest

civilian someone who is not in the armed forces

civil war war between different groups in one country

coalition government a government in which two or more parties share power

Cold War name given to the hostility that existed between the free enterprise capitalist and communist worlds between 1947 and the late 1980s

collective ownership situation in which land, property or services are owned by the population as a whole, rather than by individuals

colony a country ruled by another country

communism political theory and practice which puts the interests of society as a whole above the interests of individuals

conservative liking traditional ways and disliking change

coup violent seizure of power

covert done secretly

democracy political system that allows people an equal say in the election of their government representative

dictator ruler who has unlimited power

economic sanctions policy of refusing to trade with a particular country

empire a group of countries controlled by another more powerful country

ethnic group relating to different tribal or racial groups

fundamentalism returning to the basics of any religion or ideology, which often involves supporting what are now considered old-fashioned social and political ideas

garrison building to be occupied by troops

guerrilla tactics fighting in small groups and using surprise attacks on the enemy

hijackers people who illegally seize an aircraft or other vehicle

imperialism empire-building

infrastructure economic foundations of a society, for example roads and power supplies

intelligence service secret agency which seeks out information and tries to counter enemies of a state, both at home and abroad

interim government temporary government with the job of setting up a permanent government

irrigation system network of pipes and channels that supply water to the land so that crops can be grown

Islam one of the world's major monotheistic (one God) religions, founded by the Prophet Mohammed in the 7th century

Islamic fundamentalism *see* fundamentalism

jihad war on behalf of Islam

jirgah gathering of people for the making of decisions

KGB state security police of the USSR

land reform changing the amount of land different people own or control (in recent times, usually taking land from large landowners and giving it to those with little or no land)

literacy ability to read and write

militia a military force often made up of civilians

mujahedin Muslim guerilla fighters

mullah Islamic clergyman

Muslim follower of Islam

nation-building in recent times, re-uniting nations which have been divided by conflict

natural resources naturally occurring substances, like coal and oil, that can be used for economic gain

nuclear disarmament reduction in the number of nuclear weapons a country possesses

oath of allegiance formal swearing of loyalty

peasant small farmer, often without land

prejudice fixed opinions that are formed without fair examination of the facts

propaganda publicity that is intended to make people believe something

refugee one who flees for safety, usually to another country

revolution widespread protest that leads to a dramatic change in the government of a country

sanctuary place of safety

secular unconcerned with religion or religious identities

Security Council 15-member council within the United Nations responsible for the maintenance of world peace and security

security police police concerned with the security of the regime in power

Sharia Islamic law

Shi'a Muslims smaller of two major Muslim groups, which originated in a dispute over who should lead all Muslims

Soviet Union another name for the Union of Soviet Socialist Republics (USSR), a communist country that included Russia

suicide bomber person who deliberately blows himself or herself up in order to kill others

Sunni Muslims larger of two major Muslim groups, which originated in a dispute over who should lead all Muslims

superpower state or states which dominate the rest. The USA and the Soviet Union were the superpowers of the Cold War period (1947-89); since then, the USA has been considered the only superpower

terrain a stretch of land and especially its physical features e.g. mountainous terrain

terrorist person who uses violence and intimidation against ordinary people for political ends

unilateral decision or action taken by one person or group of people without consulting anyone else

United Nations (UN) an international organization of governments set up after World War II to promote peace and understanding between nations

warlords leaders with an armed following who control significant amounts of territory

War on Terrorism worldwide campaign led by the USA to eliminate terrorism which began in September 2001

West/Western political rather than geographical name for the rich, industrialized countries of western and northern Europe, North America, Australia and New Zealand

Index